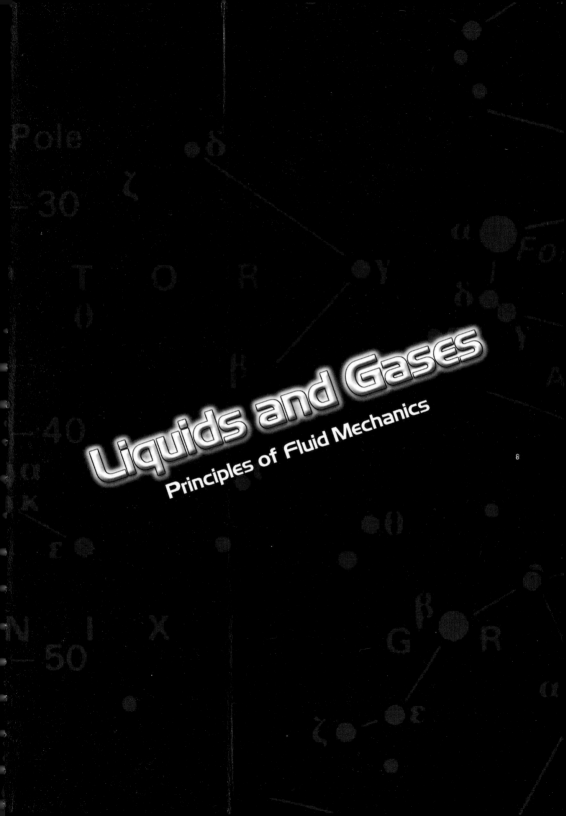

Liquids and Gases

Principles of Fluid Mechanics

Secrets of the Universe

Liquids and Gases

Principles of Fluid Mechanics

by Paul Fleisher

Lerner Publications Company · Minneapolis

For Embry

The text for this book has been adapted from a single-volume work entitled *Secrets of the Universe: Discovering the Universal Laws of Science,* by Paul Fleisher, originally published by Atheneum in 1987. Illustrations by Tim Seeley were commissioned by Lerner Publications Company. New back matter was developed by Lerner Publications Company.

Lerner Publications Company
A division of Lerner Publishing Group
241 First Avenue North
Minneapolis, MN 55401 U.S.A.

Website address: www.lernerbooks.com

Library of Congress Cataloging-in-Publication Data

Fleisher, Paul.
Liquids and gases : principles of fluid mechanics / by Paul Fleisher.
    p. cm. — (Secrets of the universe)
    Includes bibliographical references and index.
    ISBN 0-8225-2988-2 (lib. bdg. : alk. paper)
    1. Fluid mechanics—Juvenile literature. [1. Liquids. 2. Gases.] I. Title.
QC145.24.F57   2002
532–dc21   00-011785

Manufactured in the United States of America
1 2 3 4 5 6 – JR – 07 06 05 04 03 02

Contents

INTRODUCTION

Everyone knows what a law is. It's a rule that tells people what they must or must not do. Laws tell us that we shouldn't drive faster than the legal speed limit, that we must not take someone else's property, that we must pay taxes on our income each year.

What Is a Natural Law?

Where do these laws come from? In the United States and other democratic countries, laws are created by elected representatives. These men and women discuss which ideas they think would be fair and useful. Then they vote to decide which ones will actually become laws.

But there is another kind of law, a scientific law. You may have heard about Archimedes' principle, for example. It is a scientific law that tells us a floating object displaces (or pushes aside) an amount of water equal to its own weight. If the object is too heavy and dense to push aside enough water, it will sink. Where did that law come from and what could we do if we decided to change it?

Archimedes' principle is very different from a speed limit or a law that says you must pay your taxes. Speed limits are different in different places. On many interstate highways, drivers can travel 105 kilometers (65 miles) per hour. On crowded city streets, they must drive more slowly. But Archimedes' principle works exactly the same way no matter where you are. In the country or the city, in France, Brazil, or the United States, a floating object displaces its own weight.

Sometimes people break laws. When the speed limit is 88 kph (55 mph), people often drive 97 kph (60 mph) or even faster. But what happens when you try to "break" Archimedes' principle? You can't. Here on Earth, if you float one thousand different objects, each one will push aside an amount of water exactly equal to its weight.

All objects obey this law, too: plants, animals, water, stones, and even people. And we know that Archimedes' principle stays in effect whether people are watching or not.

Archimedes' principle is a natural law, or a rule of nature. Scientists and philosophers have studied events in our world for a long time. They have made careful observations and done many experiments. And they have found that certain events happen over and over again in a regular, predictable way.

You have probably noticed some of the same things yourself. Archimedes' principle is a good example. When you put an object in water, it will float or sink. Objects that are denser than water will sink. You know that from experience.

A scientific law is a statement that tells how things work in the universe. It describes the way things are, not the way we want them to be. That means a scientific law is not something that can be changed whenever we choose. We can change the speed limit or the tax rate if we think they're too high or too low. But no matter how much we want an object to float instead of sink, Archimedes' principle remains in effect. We cannot change it; we can only describe what happens. A scientist's job is to describe the laws of nature as accurately and exactly as possible.

The laws you will read about in this book are universal laws. That means they are true not only here on Earth, but elsewhere throughout the universe too. The universe includes everything we know to exist: our planet, our solar system, our galaxy, all the other billions of stars and galaxies, and all the vast empty space in between. All the evidence that scientists have gathered about the other planets and stars in our universe tells us that the scientific laws that apply here on Earth also apply everywhere else.

In the history of science, some laws have been found through the brilliant discoveries of a single person. Archimedes' principle, for example, is the result of the Greek philosopher Archimedes' great flash of individual understanding. But ordinarily, scientific laws are discovered through the efforts of many scientists, each one building on what others did earlier. When one scientist receives credit for discovering a law, it's important to remember that many other people also contributed to that discovery.

Scientific laws do change, on rare occasions, but they don't change because we tell the universe to behave differently. Scientific laws change only if we have new information or more accurate observations. The law changes when scientists make new discoveries that show the old law does not describe the universe as well as it should. Whenever scientists agree to a change in the laws of nature, the new law describes events more completely, or more simply and clearly.

For example, Aristotle—one of the founders of scientific thought—believed that air had no weight. Early scientists held that belief for almost two thousand years. Finally in the mid-1600s, the Italian scientist Evangelista Torricelli created the world's first barometer. Scientists then realized that the air at sea level does have weight—enough weight to support a column of mercury 76 centimeters (30 inches) high. Several years later, the French scientist Blaise Pascal showed that the weight of the air decreased as you climbed higher and higher.

Natural laws are often written in the language of mathematics. This allows scientists to be more exact in their descriptions of how things work. For example, the ideal gas law, which we'll learn about later in this book, is actually written like this:

$$V \text{ (volume)} = R \text{ (gas constant)} \times \frac{T \text{ (temperature)}}{P \text{ (pressure)}}$$

Don't let the math fool you. It describes the actions of air and other gases that you are familiar with in everyday life. Writing it this way lets scientists accurately compute the actual volume, temperature, or pressure of a gas in many different situations here on Earth and elsewhere in the universe.

The science of matter and energy and how they behave is called physics. In the hundreds of years that physicists have been studying our universe, they have discovered many natural laws. In this book, you'll read about some of these great discoveries. There will be some simple experiments you can do to see the laws in action. Read on, and share the fascinating stories of the laws that reveal the secrets of our universe.

CHAPTER 1

Archimedes' Principle

An oceangoing ship weighs hundreds or even thousands of tons. Yet it can float on water. How is that possible? The answer begins with one of the oldest and most famous stories in the history of science.

Let's imagine an experiment. You decide to take a bath, so you turn on the water and fill the tub to the very top. Then, with the tub filled just to overflowing, you step in and sit down.

Even without trying, you know exactly what will happen. In fact, you'd better not try it, unless you want to do a lot of mopping up afterward! When you get into the tub, gallons of water will pour onto the floor.

According to an ancient story, this is just what happened to the Greek scientist Archimedes more than 2,200 years ago. Archimedes sat down in an overly full bathtub, and water flooded over the sides. Seeing the water overflow gave Archimedes a brilliant idea. He was so excited about his new idea that he jumped out of the tub. Forgetting to put on his clothes, he ran through the streets shouting "Eureka!" ("I found it!")

Archimedes had been thinking about why some things float while others sink. It couldn't just be a matter of weight. Greek ships were very heavy, and yet they floated. But even a tiny pebble sinks right to the bottom of the sea.

What Archimedes found in his bathtub was the law of buoyancy. In modern times, this is usually known as *Archimedes' principle* in his honor. Archimedes' principle says: Any floating object pushes aside, or displaces, an amount of water equal to its own weight. If a boat weighs 250 kilograms (550 pounds), it must displace 250 kilograms of water in order to float.

Imagine a boat pushing a "hole" into the water. If you measured the amount of water it would take to fill that hole, it would weigh as much as the boat itself. A boat that weighs 100 metric tons (110 tons) must push aside 100 metric tons of water to float.

If you measure carefully, you will be able to see this law at work in the following demonstration. Place an aluminum pie plate on a sensitive scale. Weigh it and record its weight. Next, find an object that will float—like a block of wood— weigh it, and write down its weight.

Put the pie plate back on the scale. Place an empty can or wide-mouthed jar in the center of the plate. Carefully fill the jar with water to the very top. The water should be ready to overflow if you add just one more drop.

Gently lower the block of wood into the can of water until it floats by itself. Some of the water in the can will overflow as the block pushes it out of the can. That's exactly what should happen.

After the wood is floating in the can, carefully lift the whole can, with the wood and the water, out of the pie plate. Pick up the can very gently so that you don't spill any more water out of it.

Weigh the pie plate with the overflow water in it. Subtract the weight of the pie plate itself. That will give you the weight of the water that the block of wood pushed out of the can.

$$\begin{array}{r} \text{Total weight of water and pan} \\ - \ \underline{\text{Weight of pan}} \\ \text{Weight of water in pan} \end{array}$$

Compare the weight of the water in the pan to the weight of the block of wood. They should be equal. The water that the floating object displaces weighs just as much as the object itself. That's Archimedes' principle.

Archimedes' principle is true for any object, in any situation. That's why it's considered a law. If an object can displace its own weight in water, it will float. If it's too heavy or dense to displace its own weight, it will sink.

Try the same experiment using a rock instead of a block of wood. The rock will sink to the bottom. As it does, it will push some of the water out of the jar and into the pie plate. Compare the weight of the rock to the weight of the water

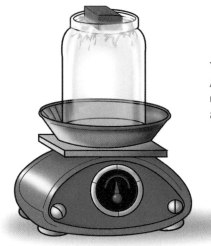

You can demonstrate Archimedes' principle using a jar, a pie plate, and a small scale.

it displaced. You should discover that the rock weighs more than the water in the pan. The rock wasn't able to displace its own weight in water, so it sank.

Archimedes' principle can be described in another way: If an object is less dense than water, it will float. If it is denser than water, it will sink.

A rock doesn't displace enough water to be able to float.

Two different objects can be exactly the same size (or volume), but one can be much heavier than the other. A brick and a block of plastic foam may be exactly the same size. But when you compare their weights, the brick is much heavier. The brick has much greater density.

The density of an object is calculated by comparing its volume with its weight. The more mass (the amount of matter or substance an object is made of) that is packed into the same amount of space, the greater the density.

Imagine comparing the weight of our block of wood with the weight of a "chunk" of water that is exactly the same size and shape as the wood. If we could weigh the block of wood and the "block" of water, the water would weigh more. That means the wood is less dense than the water, so it will float.

If we weighed a "chunk" of water the same size as our rock, we would get a different result. The rock would weigh more than the chunk of water. The rock is denser than the water, and so it sinks.

The material an object is made of has a lot to do with whether or not it will float. But as you might guess from the way boats are designed, so does an object's shape. Here's another experiment to show how true that is.

Tear off two equally sized sheets of aluminum foil. Form one into the shape of a canoe. Fold and crush the other one into a small ball, squeezing it as tightly as you can.

Place both pieces of foil in a container of water. The ball sinks right to the bottom. As long as it doesn't fill with water, the foil canoe should float. Because of its shape, the canoe can displace its own weight of water, and so it floats. The densely packed ball cannot displace enough water, and so it sinks.

A submarine is a very special kind of boat. It uses Archimedes' principle very precisely to either sink or float. A submarine has several ballast tanks in its hull. When these tanks are filled with water, the submarine weighs more than the water it displaces. It sinks toward the bottom.

The same amount of foil can be made into a floating canoe or a tight ball that will sink.

When the captain wants to float to the surface, he uses compressed air to force the water out of the tanks. This makes the submarine lighter. It then displaces more than its own weight of water, and it rises toward the surface.

To keep the submarine at a certain depth, the captain allows just enough water in the tanks to give the submarine neutral buoyancy. That means the ship weighs exactly as much as the water it displaces. It stays just where it is, neither rising nor sinking.

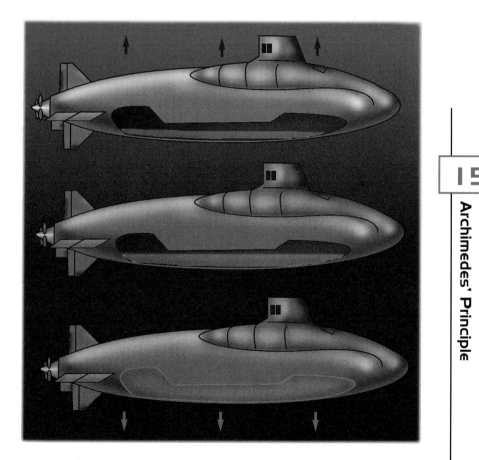

A submarine changes its buoyancy by adjustments to the amount of water in its tanks.

Archimedes' principle doesn't apply just to objects floating in water. It's true for any liquid or gas.

Helium is less dense than air. A helium-filled balloon rises in the air because it displaces more air than its own weight. A balloon filled with the heavy gas xenon will quickly sink to the ground. It weighs much more than an equal volume of air. And a heavy bar of steel will float gently on the surface of a pool of mercury, an even denser liquid metal.

Archimedes made many other noteworthy contributions to science and technology. He invented a new type of water pump. He began the science of mechanics, the study of how objects move. He explained how to use levers to move heavy loads. Although he hated war, he invented new weapons to help the Greeks defend themselves against their enemies. But the contribution for which he is best remembered still bears his name. Eureka!

CHAPTER 2

Pascal's Law—How Liquids Behave

If you are a good swimmer, you've probably tried swimming down to the bottom of a pool or lake. When you did, you certainly felt the water pushing harder on you as you swam deeper and deeper. If you were wearing goggles, you felt the water pressing them firmly against your face. Water can exert a tremendous amount of pressure. In the deepest parts of the ocean, the pressure of the water is more than 7,300 kilograms (16,000 pounds) per square inch!

Ever since the earliest civilizations, humans have needed dependable supplies of water. We need water to drink, to wash, to grow our crops, and to supply us with power. But to use water effectively, we have to learn how water behaves and how it can be controlled. We need to know the laws that explain how water flows and how water pressure works.

The study of liquids is known as hydrodynamics. The

prefix *hydro-* means "water," and *dynamics* is the study of motion. One of the earliest and most important laws of hydrodynamics is known as *Pascal's law.*

Pascal's law is named for its discoverer, Blaise Pascal, a French scientist and philosopher who lived and worked in the mid-1600s. Pascal's scientific studies focused on pressure in both liquids and gases. He was the first to prove that air pressure decreased with altitude. Pascal was weakened by illness throughout his short life, but his friends climbed high into the mountains for him and took barometer readings at different altitudes. The different measurements they recorded proved that air pressure is greatest at sea level and that it decreases as the altitude increases.

Gravity pulls the air of our atmosphere down toward the center of the Earth. Air pressure is caused by the weight of the atmosphere pressing down from above. At higher altitudes, the layer of air is thinner. There is less air pressing down, and so the air pressure is less.

Pascal knew that something very similar happens with water pressure. In any container of water, the pressure is least at the top. As you go deeper and deeper in the water, the pressure increases. The deeper you go, the more water there is pressing down from above. This is true in a drinking glass, a swimming pool, or an ocean.

To demonstrate this for yourself, all you need is an empty plastic jug. (Do this experiment in a sink!) Using a small nail, carefully punch a series of three or four holes down the side of the jug. The first hole should be near the top of the jug, and the last should be very near the bottom. Fill the jug with water and watch it squirt out of the holes. You'll see that the water barely dribbles out of the top hole. But the water coming out of the holes farther down the side spurts out more and more forcefully. The lowest hole has the strongest stream of all. That is because the water at that point is the deepest and has the greatest pressure.

Water pressure increases with the depth of the water column.

The additional pressure is caused by the weight of the water above pressing down. The amount of water above a point is known as the water column. The deeper a point is, the taller the column of water above it. The water in that column presses down with all its weight. And water is heavy! Four liters (1 gallon) of water weighs 4 kilograms (about 9 pounds). One cubic meter (a cube 1 meter [3 feet] long, 1 meter wide, and 1 meter high) of water has a mass of 1,000 kilograms (2,200 pounds).

Water pressure depends only on the depth of the water column. The total amount of water in a container and the shape of the container make no difference. At a depth of 10 meters (30 feet), there is exactly as much water pressure in a narrow pipe as in a deep lake. In the drawing on the next page, the pressure at the bottom of each container would be exactly the same.

Although the containers have different shapes, the water pressure at the bottom of each one is exactly the same.

Pascal proved this by making a container that looked like this:

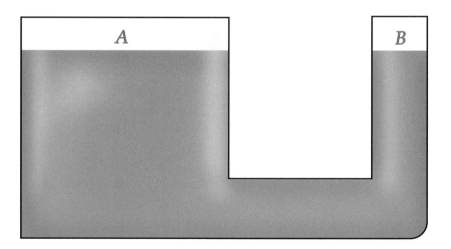

A   *B*

Pascal built a container like this to show that water pressure depends on the depth of the water, not the size or shape of the container.

You might think that section *A* would have more pressure because it contains more water than section *B*. But if section *A* had more pressure, then we would expect that pressure to push the water up higher in section *B*. When Pascal filled his container with water, the smaller column of water reached exactly the same height as the larger one. That meant that the pressures had to be equal.

If you have a teakettle or pitcher with a spout in your kitchen at home, you can perform a similar experiment. Fill the pitcher with water. The water in the spout will always be at exactly the same level as the water in the larger portion of the pitcher.

Perhaps you have heard the expression, "Water seeks its own level." Pascal's experiment shows the reason for that: Equal columns of a liquid exert equal pressures.

Water pressure at any point is directly proportional to the depth of the water at that point. The deeper the water, the greater the pressure. But Pascal found that water pressure doesn't just push downward. If that were true, then whenever we dived underwater, we would be pushed right to the bottom! That doesn't happen, of course. Water pressure pushes in all directions equally.

To demonstrate this fact, you will need a bucket and a couple of empty plastic drinking cups. Punch a hole in the bottom of one cup with a nail. Fill the bucket with water. Push the cup partway down into the water. You should see water being pushed up through the hole in the bottom of the cup.

Try the same experiment with another cup. This time punch a hole in the side of the cup. Push this cup into the water. Notice the direction that the water takes as it gushes into the cup.

Pascal noticed that the pressure of a liquid always seems to push at 90 degrees to the object it is pushing against. With the hole in the bottom of the cup, the water pushed directly up. When the hole was in the side, the water pushed in sideways. Therefore, the pressure of a liquid pushes in all directions. And it always acts at right angles to the object it pushes against.

Pascal also considered what happens when you apply additional pressure to a liquid. When pressure is applied to a gas, the gas can be compressed into a smaller space. For example, scuba divers can squeeze an hour's worth of air into a small steel tank. But liquids can't be compressed. No matter how much pressure is applied to them, liquids will not squeeze into a smaller space.

Imagine you have a container like the one on the next page. The tube on the left has a piston that can be moved up or down. What will happen when you push down on that piston? The pressure you apply will be transmitted through the water, forcing the water level in the other tube to rise.

Pascal realized that when pressure is applied to liquid in a container, that pressure doesn't remain just at the point where it is applied. The pressure is distributed evenly throughout the liquid. That rule, combined with the idea that liquid pressure pushes evenly in all directions, is known as Pascal's law. Pascal's law can be stated like this: Pressure applied to a liquid at any point in a closed container is transmitted evenly throughout the container. The pressure always exerts a force at right angles to the walls of the container.

Suppose we press down on the piston with 1 kilogram of force per square centimeter (14 pounds per square inch). That pressure is distributed evenly throughout the container. Wherever we measure the pressure of the liquid, the reading will be the same: 1 kilogram per square centimeter.

Pascal's law has some very important uses in our modern world. Imagine a container with one small piston and one large piston. Let's suppose that the small piston is 1 square centimeter (0.2 square inch) in area, and the large

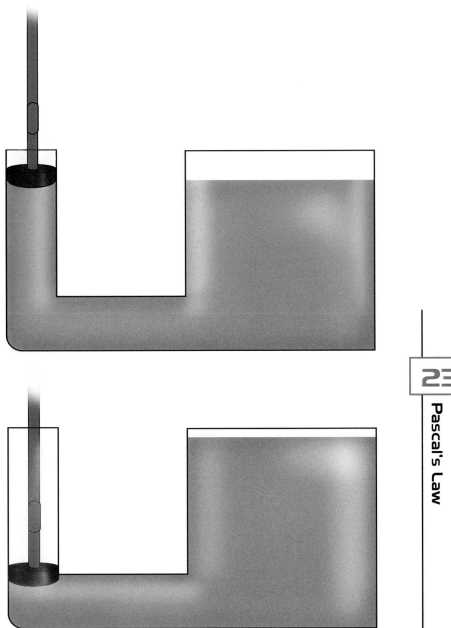

(Top) Pressure from the piston on the left will be transferred throughout the liquid. *(Bottom)* When you push down on the piston on the left, the water on the right rises.

piston has an area of 10 square centimeters (2 square inches). Then our container would look like this:

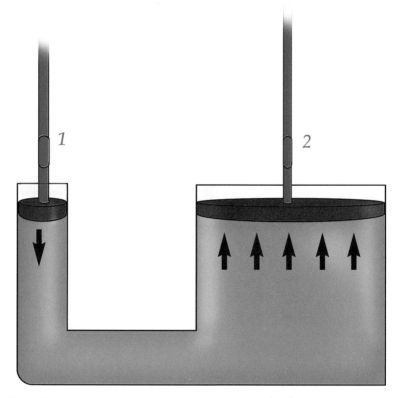

One kilogram of force on the smaller piston *(left)* is multiplied to 10 kilograms (20 pounds) of force on the larger one *(right)*.

If you push down on the small piston with 1 kilogram of force, you are exerting a pressure of 1 kilogram per square centimeter. Pascal's law tells us that the liquid in the container will transmit that amount of pressure everywhere in the container. Each square centimeter will have 1 kilogram of pressure on it.

Look at the other piston. It has an area of 10 square centimeters. Pascal's law says that pressure applied to a liquid is transmitted evenly throughout the container. So each square centimeter in our container must have 1 kilogram of pressure pushing on it. That means the large piston has a total of 10 kilograms (20 pounds) of pressure pushing on it. We could move a 10-kilogram weight using 1 kilogram of force!

You should also notice, however, that to move the large piston up 1 centimeter, you would have to push the small piston down 10 centimeters (4 inches). No work gets done for free when you follow the laws of physics!

The device we have just looked at is a simplified version of a hydraulic jack. It is used to lift heavy weights. You are most likely to see one at a garage or service station, where it is used to lift cars and trucks. A hydraulic jack uses Pascal's law to multiply a person's effort. It lets someone move a large amount of mass with only a small amount of force.

Pascal's law is also used in the braking system of every car. A car's brake system is a hydraulic system similar to the hydraulic jack. The driver's brake pedal is connected to the brakes in the wheels by long tubes. The tubes are filled with a liquid. When the driver presses down on the brake pedal, he or she pushes on a piston. That increases the pressure in the brake fluid. Pascal's law tells us that a liquid transmits pressure throughout a closed container. The liquid in the brake system transmits the pressure of the driver's foot to the brakes themselves. The brakes clamp against the turning wheel, slowing the car.

Devices like hydraulic jacks and automobile brakes don't use water to transmit pressure. When water and steel are in contact for long periods of time, the steel begins to rust. Instead, they use a kind of oil. Because the oil is a liquid, it also follows Pascal's law.

Blaise Pascal was a genius who accomplished many things in his short life. He was a noted religious philosopher. He was the first scientist to create a vacuum (a space containing no air or other matter) in the laboratory. In addition to his pressure studies, Pascal is best known for his mathematical study of probability, or chance. He also built the first mathematical counting machine. Pascal's machine is usually considered to be the first computer. In honor of that accomplishment, a modern-day computer language is named for him. And because of his achievements in the study of air and water pressure, the metric unit that is used to measure pressure is called the pascal.

CHAPTER 3

Boyle's and Charles's Laws— How Gases Behave

If you look at the directions on any aerosol spray can, you will see a warning: DO NOT INCINERATE. That means don't throw the can into a fire. If you do, the heat will turn that harmless spray can into a bomb.

What causes the heated can to explode so violently? Why does a rubber bicycle tire, when pumped with enough soft, gentle air, become firm and hard? And why does the air released from the valve of that tire always feel cold, even on the hottest day? These characteristics are explained by a set of rules commonly called gas laws.

Matter comes in three different forms, or states: solid, liquid, and gas. Most substances can exist in any of these three states, depending on their temperature. For example, water can exist as ice (solid), water (liquid), or water vapor (gas).

Each state of matter has different properties. A solid has a definite size and a definite shape. An ice cube, a brick, or a pencil holds its shape if we turn it or move it from one place to another. A liquid has a definite size but no particular shape. When we pour water or oil from one container to another, it changes shape to fit whatever container it is in. But it still takes up the same amount of space, even if we try to compress it.

A gas has the most interesting behavior of all. A gas has neither a definite shape nor a definite size. Air is a gas, of course. It can take the shape of a football, a basketball, or a bicycle tire. No matter what shape the container has, the gas will fit it.

A gas can expand to fill any size and shape of space. And a gas can be compressed into smaller volumes too. It will completely fill any container it is put in.

Picture a closed room with nothing in it, not even air. Such an empty space is called a vacuum. If we release just a small amount of air into that room, it won't stay in just one place. It will quickly spread out and fill the whole room evenly.

We can fill a container with lots and lots of gas by putting it under pressure. You have certainly seen pressurized canisters of helium gas. We can then use the gas in one small container to fill hundreds of helium balloons. All together, the balloons take up much more space than the canister. But the balloons and the canister were filled with the same amount of gas.

In the late 1600s, the English scientist Robert Boyle invented an air pump. This pump could increase or decrease the amount of gas in a container. The pump could even remove almost all the air from a container, creating a vacuum.

Boyle noticed that gas seemed to be "springy." The smaller the space he squeezed it into, the more pressure the gas had. He discovered there was an exact relationship between the pressure of a gas and the volume of space it was squeezed into.

Picture a container of air. Imagine that we can compress the container of air to make it smaller, without any of the air inside escaping. If we compressed the container to half of its original size, the pressure of the air inside would be twice as great. If we squeezed the container to one-third of its original size, the pressure would be three times as great. Boyle also noticed that this rule is true only as long as the temperature of the gas is kept the same.

Boyle's law is usually stated like this: At a constant temperature, the volume of a gas is inversely proportional to its pressure. "Inversely proportional" means that as the pressure on the gas increases, the volume decreases.

We often see Boyle's law at work in our everyday world. Boyle's law explains why a bicycle pump works. As

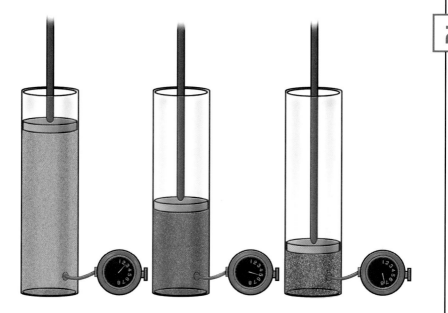

When the same amount of gas is squeezed into an increasingly small space, its pressure increases.

you push down on the handle of a bicycle pump, the air inside is forced into a smaller and smaller space. As the air's volume decreases, its pressure increases. This increased pressure forces the air out of the pump's nozzle and into the tire you are inflating.

Boyle's law also explains why basketballs and tennis balls are bouncy. The balls are filled with pressurized gas. When a basketball hits the floor, the bottom of the ball is pushed in slightly. That increases the pressure in the ball because there is less space for the air inside. The pressure of the air pushes back against the flexible wall of the ball, making it spring back into the air.

Boyle's law is even responsible for our breathing. When we breathe in, a muscle called the diaphragm moves. This increases the volume of our lungs. The extra volume means that our lungs have less air pressure than the outside air. The outside air, which has more pressure, rushes in to fill the extra space. When we breathe out, the diaphragm decreases the volume of our lungs. That raises the pressure, forcing the air to rush out again.

Here's how to make a scientific toy called a Cartesian diver. The Cartesian diver is named after the great French philosopher and mathematician René Descartes. It works because of Boyle's law, along with Pascal's law and Archimedes' principle.

To make a Cartesian diver, you'll need a drinking glass; a tall, narrow-mouthed, clear plastic bottle, like a 2-liter (0.5 gallon) soda bottle; and a medicine dropper. If you don't have a medicine dropper at home, you should be able to buy one at any drugstore.

Fill both the drinking glass and the bottle almost to the top with water. Carefully fill the medicine dropper with just enough water so that it barely floats at the surface of the water in the drinking glass. If you use too much water, the dropper will sink. (That's why you should try it out in the drinking glass first, before you put it into the bottle.) If you

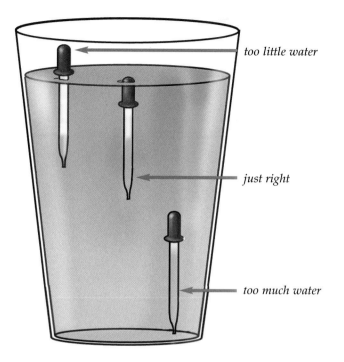

too little water

just right

too much water

For a Cartesian diver to work, it must have just the right amount of water in it.

use too little water, you won't be able to make the dropper dive. Add or remove a few drops of water at a time until the diver floats, as shown in the diagram above.

Once you have the right amount of water in the dropper, transfer it to the tall plastic bottle full of water. Be careful not to lose any water by squeezing the rubber bulb as you pick it up. Then tighly screw the top onto the bottle.

Squeeze the sides of the bottle with your hands. The medicine dropper should dive to the bottom of the bottle. It will stay there as long as you keep the pressure on the sides of the bottle. When you release the pressure, the diver will rise back to the surface.

It may take a little practice before you can make your

diver move up and down, but once you get the hang of it, it's easy! You can even make the diver float in the middle of the bottle, if you adjust the pressure of your hands correctly.

The Cartesian diver works because of three laws: The first is Pascal's law. Remember that liquids cannot be compressed into smaller spaces the way gases can. Pascal's law says that when pressure is applied to a liquid, the pressure is transmitted evenly in all directions throughout the liquid. That means that when you squeeze the bottle, pressure increases everywhere inside the bottle.

Watch the diver very closely as you make it dive and sink several times. You should notice something interesting happening to the water level inside the dropper. When you apply pressure, a little more water goes up into the dropper. When you release the pressure, the water level in the dropper goes back down again. The pressure from your hands is transmitted through the water and pushes on the air in the dropper.

Boyle's law tells us that when the pressure on a gas increases, its volume decreases. The water, pressing on the air in the dropper, squeezes the air into a smaller space. That allows a little more water to enter the dropper.

When water enters the dropper, the dropper becomes slightly heavier. It becomes denser than the water around it, so it sinks (Archimedes' principle). When we release the pressure, the "springiness" of the air pushes the water back out again. Then the dropper is slightly lighter, just enough to float back up.

A second rule about the behavior of gases was discovered about one hundred years after Boyle's law. It is known as *Charles's law,* after its first discoverer, the French scientist Jacques-Alexandre-César Charles. Charles was interested in scientific explorations through ballooning. He realized that gases expand when heated. In fact, that is what allows a hot-air balloon to rise.

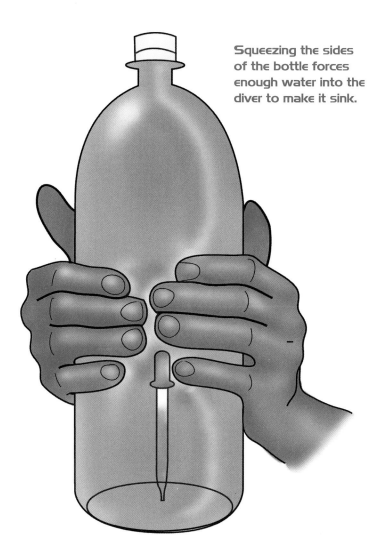

Squeezing the sides of the bottle forces enough water into the diver to make it sink.

Although it was Charles who first noticed that gases expand with heat, it was actually two other scientists who first stated the law that has been named after him. Those scientists were the Englishman John Dalton and the Frenchman Joseph-Louis Gay-Lussac. Charles's law is usually stated: If the volume of a gas remains constant, the pressure of the gas is directly proportional to its temperature.

"Directly proportional" means that as the temperature of a gas increases, its pressure also increases. Charles's law also tells us that if the pressure of the gas stays the same, the volume will increase when the gas is heated.

It's easy to see Charles's law in action. You will need a rubber balloon and a tall glass bottle. Slip the mouth of the balloon over the mouth of the bottle, making a tight seal. Warm the bottle by holding it in a pan of hot water. Watch what happens to the balloon.

As the air in the bottle is warmed *(left)*, it expands. Cooling the air in the bottle *(right)* causes it to contract.

It begins to inflate! As the temperature of the air in the bottle increases, its pressure increases. The extra pressure pushes some of the air out into the balloon, inflating it.

Take the bottle out of the hot water and allow it to cool. As the air in the bottle cools, the pressure drops and the balloon deflates. Try putting the bottle in a pan full of ice or in the freezer. What do you think should happen? As the air in the bottle gets colder and colder, the pressure continues to decrease. The outside air pressure, which is greater, pushes the balloon into the bottle.

Charles's law explains why an aerosol container in a fire is so dangerous. The pressure of the gases inside the can increases as the can gets hotter and hotter. Finally the can isn't strong enough to hold the pressure anymore, and it explodes.

Something very similar happens inside a gasoline engine. In each cylinder, gasoline is mixed with air and then ignited with a spark. The gasoline explodes, creating a very rapid rise in temperature. The gases in the cylinder also expand rapidly because of the heat. This expansion provides the force that pushes the piston in the cylinder, providing the engine's power.

Automobile manuals always instruct drivers to check the air pressure in their tires when they are cold. As a car rolls along the highway, the friction of the tires against the road creates heat. Charles's law tells us that as the tires get hotter, the pressure of the air inside them increases. When the car stops and the tires cool off, the pressure goes back down again.

A blowout is caused when a weakened tire can't hold the pressure of the air inside it. Blowouts almost always happen while a car is moving rapidly. The friction of rapid motion heats up the tires. That's when the pressure inside the tire is the greatest, according to Charles's law.

In 1824, Gay-Lussac and another French scientist, Sadi Carnot, realized that Boyle's law and Charles's law could be combined. They put the two laws together to make what is known as the *ideal gas law*. The ideal gas law says: The volume of a gas is directly proportional to its temperature and inversely proportional to its pressure. To figure out the volume of a gas, you need to know both its temperature and its pressure. In mathematical form, it looks like this:

$$\text{volume} = R \times \frac{\text{temperature}}{\text{pressure}} \quad \text{or} \quad V = R \times \frac{T}{P}$$

R stands for a special number called the gas constant, which must be used to get exact measurements from the formula. The ideal gas law simply says that the volume of a gas increases as the temperature increases, and the volume decreases as the pressure increases.

This law has a very familiar and important use in our everyday lives. It is the reason our refrigerators, freezers, and air conditioners all work.

Have you ever touched the base of a bicycle pump after you have pumped up a tire? It is very hot. You may also have noticed that when you let air out of a bicycle or car tire, it always feels cold, even on the hottest day. If you have not felt cool air coming out of a tire valve, try it the next time you check the tires of your bike or family car at a service station.

The ideal gas law tells us that when we force a gas into a smaller space, its temperature increases. It's the hot, compressed air that makes the bottom of the bicycle pump so hot. The ideal gas law also tells us that when the pressure on a gas is decreased, the temperature of the gas decreases. That's why the air released from a tire always feels cool.

Picture a gas-pumping machine with two parts. One part compresses the gas, making it hotter. The other part releases the pressure, allowing it to cool. That is a refrigerator. Every refrigerator has tubes called coils. In some refrigerators and freezers, you can see the coils. They are the winding metal tubes often covered with frost. In these coils, a pressurized gas is allowed to release its pressure. When that happens, the gas becomes cooler. This takes place inside an insulated box that we call the refrigerator. As the gas gets cooler, it absorbs heat and cools whatever is in the box too.

After the gas has cooled the inside of the refrigerator, it is pumped outside the insulated box. There a machine called a compressor, driven by an electric motor, repressurizes the gas. As the gas is pressurized, it gets hotter. But since the compressor is outside the insulated box, the heat

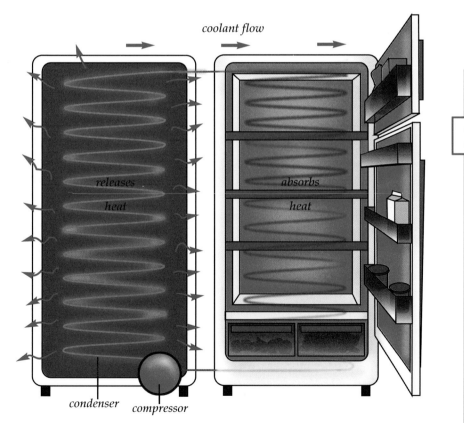

Compressed gas in the coils removes heat from the insulated refrigerator and releases it into the surrounding air via the compressor.

doesn't warm the food back up. Instead, the excess heat that the gas absorbed inside the refrigerator is picked up by the surrounding air. Usually a small fan keeps air circulating around the compressor to take away the heat. The repressurized gas is then circulated back inside the refrigerator for more cooling.

If you get close enough to your refrigerator, you should be able to hear the compressor motor running and feel the heat that has been removed from the pressurized gas. Freezers and air conditioners work in exactly the same way. They are all heat pumps. Thanks to the ideal gas law, they pump heat out of an area to be cooled and into the surrounding air.

Boyle's law and Charles's law were important in the history of science because they provided strong evidence for the existence of atoms. Here's why: Scientists picture a gas as made up of many tiny moving particles, or molecules. As gas molecules are packed closer together in a smaller space, it makes sense that more of them collide with the walls of their container. More tiny collisions result in more pressure. Boyle's law tells us that this is exactly what happens. A gas increases in pressure when its volume is decreased.

In the 1800s, scientists also realized that heat energy is actually the motion of atoms and molecules. The hotter a substance is, the faster its particles move. Charles's law supports this idea. The faster the gas molecules are moving, the harder their collisions with the walls of their container should be. Harder collisions produce more pressure. And that is exactly what happens. As a gas gets hotter, it does have more pressure.

In 1860, the British scientist James Clerk Maxwell showed that Boyle's law and Charles's law resulted from the motion of gas molecules. This proved that heat is the energy of molecular motion. The hotter something is, the faster its molecules move.

One other result of the gas laws is also very important and interesting. Starting at 0° Celsius (32° Fahrenheit), any gas loses 1/273 of its volume for each degree it is cooled. Since heat is actually the motion of molecules, that means that when a gas is cooled 1 degree, it loses 1/273 of its molecular motion.

In 1848, William Thomson (Lord Kelvin) realized that if a gas were cooled to −273°C (−460°F), its molecules would stop moving completely! That temperature, at which all motion stops, is called absolute zero. As far as we know, there is no upper limit to how hot matter can get. But Lord Kelvin proved that there is a limit to coldness. At −273°C, all molecules stop moving. Matter just can't get any colder than that.

CHAPTER 4

Bernoulli's Principle

Did you ever wonder how an airplane gets off the ground? A big jetliner weighs hundreds of thousands of pounds. How can something that heavy manage to fly? The answer is *Bernoulli's principle,* a law discovered by the Swiss mathematician Daniel Bernoulli in 1738.

To see Bernoulli's principle in action, cut a strip from a page of a newspaper. The strip should be about 5 centimeters (2 inches) wide and at least 30 centimeters (1 foot) long. Hold one end of the paper strip just below your lips and blow lightly over the paper.

You probably expected the paper to be forced down by your breath, but instead, the paper rose! That's Bernoulli's principle at work. Bernoulli's principle says that the pressure of a gas or liquid decreases as its velocity increases.

In the experiment you just tried, the air above the paper was moving fast because you were blowing. The air below the strip of paper was still. That means the moving air above the paper had less pressure than the air below it. Since there was more pressure below the paper than above it, the paper was pushed upward.

The same principle that caused the paper to rise also gives airplanes their lift. If you look at a cross-section of an airplane wing, it looks like this:

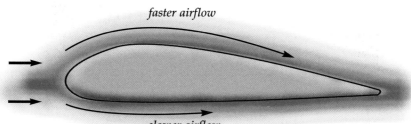

faster airflow

slower airflow

This special shape gives airplane wings their lift.

This special shape is called an airfoil. As the wing moves through the air, some air passes over the wing and some passes under it. Because the airfoil is curved on top, the air passing over the wing has a longer distance to travel in the same amount of time. That means it has to move slightly faster than the air passing underneath the wing.

Bernoulli's principle tells us that when a gas moves faster, it has less pressure. Since air is moving faster over the wing than under it, there is less pressure above and more pressure below. That gives the wing lift. If the airplane has been designed correctly, it gives enough lift to get the plane off the ground and keep it airborne.

Moving the plane forward forces air to blow over the wings and creates that lift. The force that moves a jet airplane forward comes as a result of the engine pushing huge quantities of exhaust gases backward. As a reaction, the plane goes forward. As it moves faster and faster, the wind blowing over the wings finally creates enough lift to get the plane off the ground.

Bernoulli's principle works just as well with liquids. Most chemistry labs have a piece of equipment called an aspirator. Chemists use an aspirator when they need small amounts of suction. An aspirator attaches to a water faucet and looks like this:

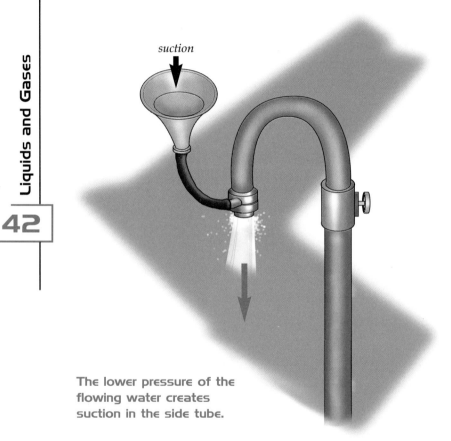

suction

The lower pressure of the flowing water creates suction in the side tube.

When the water is turned on, it rushes past the side tube at a high speed. According to Bernoulli's principle, high velocity creates low pressure. So the side tube generates suction as air or liquid flows in the direction of the arrows toward the low pressure area. If you put your finger at the end of the side tube, you would be able to feel the suction created by this pressure difference.

For another demonstration of Bernoulli's principle, you'll need a strong blow-dryer and a table-tennis ball. Plug in the dryer, turn it on high, and gently place the table-tennis ball in the stream of air.

The moving air should hold the table-tennis ball securely in place. You should be able to tilt the stream of air over to one side and still support the ball in the airstream. It looks as if gravity should make the ball fall, but instead the ball hangs mysteriously in midair.

Try it. Can you figure out what is holding the ball in place?

The table-tennis ball is surrounded by a column of rapidly moving air. That air has low pressure, according to Bernoulli's principle. The moving air is surrounded by air with higher pressure. Whenever the ball starts to move out of the moving air column, the higher pressure in the surrounding air pushes it back. The ball is light enough and the pressure difference is strong enough to overcome the force of gravity for a time. Gravity is still working, of course. It's just that in this case, the air pressure is stronger. The same thing is true every time a huge jetliner lifts off a runway.

Science now understands many of the rules that govern the movement of liquids and gases. But we still don't know all there is to know about the universe. Scientists still have much to learn about the stars and planets, the atom, and the miracles of life. There are still more laws to discover and more mysteries to solve. Perhaps you may one day add your name to that distinguished list of scientists who have helped discover the secrets of the universe.

c. 287 B.C.	Archimedes' birth
A.D. 1624	Jan Baptista van Helmont first uses the word "gas" to describe a state of matter other than solid or liquid
c. 1643	Evangelista Torricelli invents and builds the first mercury barometer to measure atmospheric pressure
c. 1648	**Blaise Pascal develops Pascal's law of fluid pressure**
c. 1650	Otto von Guericke develops a working air pump
1661	Robert Boyle publishes *The Sceptical Chymist*
1687	Isaac Newton publishes his *Principia*
1692	Witchcraft trials take place in Salem, MA
1738	**Daniel Bernoulli publishes *Hydrodynamica*, which presents Bernoulli's principle**
1755	Samuel Johnson's *Dictionary of the English Language* is published
1772	Daniel Rutherford discovers nitrogen
1774	Joseph Priestley discovers oxygen
1775–1783	American War of Independence
1783	Jacques-Alexandre-César Charles makes the first manned flight in a hydrogen balloon
1787	U.S. Constitution is signed
1789	George Washington becomes the first president of the United States

1799	The Rosetta Stone is discovered in Egypt
1808	John Dalton proposes that every element is made up of atoms
1811	Amedeo Avogadro proposes his gas law
1824	**Boyle's and Charles's laws combined to make the ideal gas law**
1829	Louis Braille's system of writing for the blind is first published (revised in 1837)
1848	**William Thomson (Lord Kelvin) proposes the existence of absolute zero (–273°C), the temperature at which all molecular motion stops**
1851	Isaac Merritt Singer patents his sewing machine
1859	Charles Darwin publishes *On the Origin of Species by Means of Natural Selection*
1860	**James Clerk Maxwell's study of gases shows the relationship between heat and molecular motion**
1861–1865	American Civil War
1865	President Abraham Lincoln is assassinated
1873	Johannes Diderik van der Waals publishes his equations, which more accurately describe the behavior of gases than does the ideal gas law
1876	Alexander Graham Bell patents his telephone
1903	The Wright brothers make the first manned airplane flight
1937	The *Hindenburg* explodes
1939	First successful flight of a jet-engine airplane

Archimedes
(c. 287–212 B.C.) was a mathematician and physicist from Syracuse, a Greek colony in Sicily. His many discoveries and inventions and his work in mathematics make him one of the most important figures in early science. The compound pulley and the principle of the lever are two of his major contributions. He may be best known for discovering the law of buoyancy, also known as Archimedes' principle. The son of an astronomer named Phidias, he was probably introduced to science and mathematics at a young age. Toward the end of his life, Archimedes created many inventive weapons to defend Syracuse against Roman invaders. When Syracuse was captured, Archimedes was killed by a Roman soldier.

Daniel Bernoulli
(1700–1782) was a Swiss mathematician. Bernoulli enjoyed math but also had many other interests. He originally studied medicine, but during his career he worked as a professor of math, anatomy, botany, and physics. He taught at a university in Russia for several years but didn't like the cold weather and returned to Switzerland. He did a great deal of work with both liquids and gases in many different forms. For example, he investigated blood pressure and flow, ocean currents, and the tides. His most famous discovery, Bernoulli's principle, is an idea that can be observed in the uplift of an airplane's wings.

Robert Boyle
(1627–1691) was the seventh of fourteen children born to the Earl of Cork in Ireland. Boyle grew up in a castle, went to school in England and Switzerland, and traveled to France and Italy. He finally settled in England, where he did many experiments studying

air and its properties. With the help of physicist Robert Hooke, he developed and built an improved air pump. This tool helped Boyle prove that sound cannot travel in a vacuum and that a flame needs air in order to burn. In 1660, he published a work on the relationship between the volume of a gas and its pressure, which eventually became known as Boyle's law. In 1661, he published *The Sceptical Chymist*. This work was an important step toward establishing chemistry as its own field, distinct from the other sciences.

Sadi Carnot (1796–1832) came from a very political French family. His father served as Napoleon's minister of war, and his nephew would become the president of France. Especially interested in steam engines, Carnot's studies of their efficiency proved that, even under ideal conditions, all machines must lose some energy in the form of heat. Carnot's work was not very well known during his lifetime, but his observations would be used to develop the second law of thermodynamics, also known as the law of entropy. He is considered one of the founders of thermodynamics.

Jacques-Alexandre-César Charles (1746–1823) was a French physicist with a passion for hot-air ballooning and an interest in the science of gases. From modest beginnings as an office clerk, in 1783 Charles became the first person to make a flight in a hydrogen balloon. Charles continued to study the behavior of gases, and in 1787 he developed Charles's law, which describes the relationship between the pressure and the temperature of a gas. Because Joseph-Louis Gay-Lussac later published a more complete explanation of the law, it is sometimes known as Gay-Lussac's law. Charles also studied electricity and worked as a professor of physics in Paris.

John Dalton (1766–1844) was a British scientist who began teaching when he was just twelve years old. His interests were broad, ranging from meteorology to color blindness. Color-blind himself, Dalton even requested that his eyes be donated to scientific research after his death. In the area of meteorology, he was particularly interested in rainfall and atmospheric humidity. Dalton also studied gases, contributing to the theory that was eventually formulated in Charles's law, but his most famous work was his atomic theory, stated in 1808.

Joseph-Louis Gay-Lussac (1778–1850) was a French physicist and chemist who grew up during the French Revolution. Both the political troubles in his homeland and his adventurous approach to science kept Gay-Lussac's life interesting. Like Jacques Charles before him, Gay-Lussac was very interested in hot-air ballooning. He used these trips to observe magnetism and air composition at different altitudes. Also like Charles, much of Gay-Lussac's most important work was done in the study of gases. Gay-Lussac also studied elements and chemical compounds, including a few with explosive properties. One ill-fated experiment destroyed most of his lab and left him temporarily blind.

James Clerk Maxwell (1831–1879) was a Scottish physicist and mathematician who was educated in Edinburgh, Scotland, and Cambridge, England. He was often teased as a child and grew up to be a rather shy adult, but he was one of the most brilliant scientists in history. He studied a variety of subjects such as color blindness, photography, and the rings of Saturn. He also made important contributions to the kinetic theory of gases, relating the temperature of a gas to the movement of its molecules. However, he is best known for his many important discoveries in electromagnetism

(Maxwell's equations), which proved once and for all the connection between magnetic and electrical fields. Based on these equations, he theorized that visible light is just a tiny part of a much broader spectrum of electromagnetic radiation.

Blaise Pascal (1623–1662) was a French mathematician, scientist, and philosopher. As a child, he was educated by his father and showed great talent in mathematics. As a young man, he designed and built a calculating machine for his father, who worked for the local tax court. When Pascal got older, he began studying physics. He was especially interested in fluids (liquids and gases) and pressure. He studied the differences in air pressure at different altitudes and discovered Pascal's law, which states that pressure applied to a contained liquid is constant in all directions. Toward the end of his life, Pascal, who was a devout member of the Jansenist sect of the Roman Catholic Church, wrote several religious and philosophical works.

William Thomson (Lord Kelvin) (1824–1907) was a British physicist with a wide range of interests and talents. The son of a mathematics professor, Thomson was encouraged to pursue science and began studying it at the age of ten. He eventually became a professor of physics at the University of Glasgow in Scotland, and kept the job for fifty-three years. Thomson studied subjects from magnetism to the tides, but one of his main interests was heat. His work formed a big part of the second law of thermodynamics. He was also lucky enough to make a good living in science through his work on the first operational transatlantic telegraph cable. The success of this project brought him both the title of baron and great wealth.

Asimov, Isaac. *Asimov's Chronology of Science and Discovery.* New York: HarperCollins, 1994.

Farndon, John. *Oxygen.* Tarrytown, NY: Benchmark Books, 1999.

Friedhoffer, Robert. *Physics Lab in the Home.* New York: Franklin Watts, 1997.

Henderson, Harry, and Lisa Yount. *The Scientific Revolution.* San Diego: Lucent Books, 1996.

Meadows, Jack. *The Great Scientists.* New York: Oxford University Press, 1997.

Newmark, Ann. *Chemistry.* New York: Dorling Kindersley, 1993.

Spangenburg, Ray. *The History of Science from the Ancient Greeks to the Scientific Revolution.* New York: Facts on File, 1993.

Uehling, Mark D. *The Story of Hydrogen.* New York: Franklin Watts, 1995.

Wilkinson, Philip, and Michael Pollard. *Scientists Who Changed the World.* New York: Chelsea House Publishers, 1994.

Wood, Robert W. *Who?: Famous Experiments for the Young Scientist.* Philadelphia: Chelsea House Publishers, 1999.

Websites

Center for History of Physics, sponsored by the American
    Institute of Physics
<http://www.aip.org/history/index.html>

The Franklin Institute Science Museum online
<http://www.fi.edu/tfi/welcome.html>

Kid's Castle, sponsored by the Smithsonian Institution
    Includes a science site.
<http://www.kidscastle.si.edu/>

NPR's *Sounds Like Science* site
<http://www.npr.org/programs/science/>

PBS's *A Science Odyssey* site
<http://www.pbs.org/wgbh/aso/>

Science Learning Network
<http://www.sln.org/>

Science Museum of Minnesota
<http://www.smm.org/>

For Further Reading

Adler, Irving. *The Wonders of Physics: An Introduction to the Physical World.* New York: Golden Press, 1966.

Asimov, Isaac. *Asimov's New Guide to Science.* New York: Basic Books, 1984.

Galant, Roy A. *Explorers of the Atom.* New York: Doubleday, 1974.

Goldstein-Jackson, Kevin. *Experiments with Everyday Objects: Science Activities for Children, Parents and Teachers.* Englewood Cliffs, NJ: Prentice-Hall, 1978.

Kent, Amanda, and Alan Ward. *Introduction to Physics.* Tulsa, OK: Usborne Publishing, Ltd., 1983.

Millar, David, Ian Millar, John Millar, and Margaret Millar. *The Cambridge Dictionary of Scientists.* New York: Cambridge University Press, 1996.

Narlikar, Jayant V. *The Lighter Side of Gravity.* New York: W. H. Freeman, 1982.

Nourse, Alan E. *Universe, Earth, and Atom: The Story of Physics.* New York: Harper & Row, 1969.

Rosenfeld, Sam. *Science Experiments with Water.* Irvington-on-Hudson, NY: Harvey House, 1965.

Ruchlis, Hy. *Bathtub Physics.* New York: Harcourt, Brace and World, 1967.

Silverberg, Robert. *Four Men Who Changed the Universe.* New York: G. P. Putnam's Sons, 1968.

Westphal, Wilhelm H. *Physics Can Be Fun.* Alexandria, VA: Hawthorne Books, 1965.

Wilson, Mitchell. *Seesaws to Cosmic Rays: A First View of Physics.* New York: Lothrop, Lee & Shepard, 1967.

Archimedes' principle: any floating object pushes aside, or displaces, an amount of water equal to its own weight

Bernoulli's principle: the pressure of a gas or liquid decreases as its velocity increases

Boyle's law: at a constant temperature, the volume of a gas is inversely proportional to its pressure

Charles's law: if the volume of a gas remains constant, the pressure of the gas is directly proportional to its temperature

density: a measure of the amount of mass an object contains compared to its size. Density is calculated by dividing an object's mass by its volume.

ideal gas law: the volume of a gas is directly proportional to its temperature and inversely proportional to its pressure

mass: the amount of matter an object or substance is made of

matter: any material—solid, liquid, or gas

Pascal's law: pressure applied to a liquid at any point in a closed container is transmitted evenly throughout the container

physics: the study of matter and energy and how they behave

scientific law: a statement that describes how things work in the universe

volume: the amount of space occupied by a three-dimensional object

engine, gasoline, 35

freezers. *See* refrigerators

gas, compression of, 22,
    28–30
gas constant (*R*), 36
gas laws, 27
Gay-Lussac, Joseph-Louis,
    33, 35, 48

heat. *See* molecular motion
hydraulic jack, 25
hydrodynamics (study of
    liquids), 17–18

ideal gas law, 9, 36

Kelvin, Lord. *See*
    Thompson, William

liquids, transmission of
    pressure, 22–25

mathematics, 9
matter, states of (solid,
    liquid, gas), 27–28
Maxwell, James Clerk, 38,
    48
molecular motion (heat),
    38–39

Pascal, Blaise, 9, 18, 25–26,
    49

Pascal's law, 18–25
    and Cartesian diver,
        32–33
    stated, 22

refrigerators, 36–38

scientific law, 6–8
submarines, buoyancy of,
    14–15

Thompson, William (Lord
    Kelvin), 39, 49
Torricelli, Evangelista, 8

vacuum, 25, 28

water, weight of, 19
water pressure:
    in deep ocean, 17
    increasing with depth,
        18–21
    and Pascal's law, 18–22
    pushing in all directions,
        21–22

About the Author

Paul Fleisher has written more than twenty books for young people and educators, including *Life Cycles of a Dozen Diverse Creatures*, the *Webs of Life* series, and *Brain Food*. His most recent books are *Gorillas* and *Ice Cream Treats: The Inside Scoop*. Paul is a regular contributor to *Technology and Learning* magazine. He has also created several pieces of educational software, including the award-winning *Perplexing Puzzles*.

Paul has taught in Programs for the Gifted in Richmond, Virginia, since 1978. He is also active in civic organizations that work for peace and social justice. In 1988, he received the Virginia Education Association's Award for Peace and International Relations, and in 1999 he was awarded the Thomas Jefferson Medal for Outstanding Contributions to Natural Science Education. In his spare time, you may find Paul walking through the woods, gardening, or fishing on the Chesapeake Bay. Paul and his wife, Debra Sims Fleisher, live in Richmond, Virginia.